J   21661
                                     9.95

DATE DUE

AG 20 '98			
MR 04 '99			
AP 14 '99			
MY 11 '99			
AG 23 '99			
AP 08 '00			

SOCCER

How to Play the All-Star Way

by **Barry Wilner**

Introduction by **Bobby Charlton**

Illustrated by **Art Seiden**

Photographs by **The Photo Shoppe**

★ An **Arvid Knudsen** book ★

RSVP

**RAINTREE
STECK-VAUGHN**
P U B L I S H E R S
The Steck-Vaughn Company

Austin, Texas

Dedication

To four very talented and enlightened players Nicole, Jamie, Tricia, and Evan: keep making us proud of you, on and off the field. And to Helene, the best coach and wife around, the biggest thanks of all.

Acknowledgments

I would like to thank the North Rockland Soccer Association and all of its members for their cooperation and help in compiling the information for this book. And many thanks go to all of the young players who provided the inspiration and much of the material within these covers.

For the photographs, my thanks go to The Photo Shoppe of West Haverstraw, New York. Also of particular help were Ron Blum, Alex Yannis, and Jim Trecker. Special acknowledgments go to Philip Madonia, Tony Signore, Howard Dolgon, Alan Taylor, and, of course, Bobby Charlton, one of the great gentlemen of the game. Photograph p. 8 © by FOCUS ON SPORTS

Published by Raintree/Steck-Vaughn Publishers, an imprint of Steck-Vaughn Company

Library of Congress Cataloging-in-Publication Data

Wilner, Barry.
Soccer/by Barry Wilner; introd. by Bobby Charlton; illustrations by Art Seiden; photographs by the Photo Shoppe.
p.   cm. — (How to play the all-star way)
"An Arvid Knudsen book."
Includes bibliographical references (p.   ) and index.
ISBN 0-8114-5777-X hardcover library binding
ISBN 0-8114-6343-5 softcover binding
1. Soccer—Juvenile literature. [1. Soccer.]
I. Seiden, Art, ill. II. Title. III. Series.
GV943.25.W55   1994
796.334—dc20   93-1525   CIP   AC

Printed and bound in the United States

2 3 4 5 6 7 8 9 0   99 98 97 96 95 94

CONTENTS

Introduction by Bobby Charlton . . . 4

1. A Bit of Soccer History . . . 7

2. Joining a Soccer Team . . . 9

3. Conditioning and Warm-ups . . . 13

4. The Eleven Positions . . . 17

5. Playing Skills and Techniques . . . 29

6. Playing the Game . . . 36

7. Thinking Soccer . . . 43

Find Out More . . . 45

Glossary . . . 46

More Words to Know . . . 47

Further Reading . . . 47

Index . . . 48

Bobby Charlton played in 106 international soccer games for England and scored 49 goals for his team. He was a star on England's 1966 World Cup championship team. Charlton is considered to be one of the greatest soccer players of all time. As one of the outstanding representatives of the game on the international scene, he works as a television commentator for the British Broadcasting Corporation.

INTRODUCTION

Thanks to soccer, I have been able to travel the world, meet kings and queens and presidents. I even had the thrill of carrying the World Cup around Wembley Stadium when England won the championship in 1966.

Soccer has been good to me, you see. It is a wonderful game, a game I have played all my life and have loved all my life.

I began playing when I was very young, about 3 years old, just kicking the ball around the yard or in the street. Every kid in England plays soccer, just as I hope every youngster in the United States someday will do.

When you are a good player, and I soon could claim to be quite good, you join local clubs. By the time I was in my early teens, I was playing against the best of my age in England. A few years later, I had moved to the top levels of soccer in my country and was selected to represent England in international tournaments.

Through soccer, I have played in many of the greatest sporting events, including English league championships, European Cup and club competitions and, best of all, the World Cup. I have been on teams that have won them all.

Everywhere I have traveled, I see the goalposts and the field, and I know that the youngsters in that city or that country are playing the game. It is a sport that brings all of us closer together.

Soccer truly has become an international sport. The World Cup is coming to the United States in 1994, and there is talk of playing it someday soon in China, Japan, and Africa.

This book offers an excellent and entertaining way to learn the great game of soccer. Soccer can be very simple when you start with the basic skills and build from there. I hope *Soccer: How to Play the All-Star Way* by Barry Wilner will help young players do just that. Who knows? Maybe one day they will be able to share some of these great experiences.

> **— By Bobby Charlton**
> Forward and midfielder,
> England's 1966 World Cup Champions

A BIT OF SOCCER HISTORY

Soccer, under many different names, has been part of sports in nearly every nation for years. They played it long ago in China. They played it in ancient Greece and all over the Roman Empire.

Modern soccer began in England. It was popular with children in the London streets in the 1100s. In the 1300s, soccer was banned in England. It was not played there again for nearly 400 years.

One English king who banned soccer was Richard II. He wanted the men in his country to be archery experts. He told them to practice with bow and arrow so they could defend England against its enemies.

By the 1500s, soccer was back. Soon, it was the most popular sport in England. Called football there, it became so popular in schools that every young boy in England was expected to play.

The word *soccer* came after the London Football Association insisted the sport have its own name. The association did not want the game of soccer confused with rugby, for example.

In rugby, players can use their hands and arms. The players in soccer can use only their feet. So they called their game association

◄ Superstar Mark Van Basten of Holland scores in
the European Championship.

football. Soon, people were shortening the name to "assoc." Eventually, the word *soccer* developed.

By 1863, the association had a set of rules. In general, those rules are used today as the laws of the game. The game is the number one sport in just about every nation in the world. The World Cup, the championship tournament for all soccer, is the most popular sporting event. It was watched on television by more than one billion people in 1990.

Soccer is not as popular in the United States as basketball, football, and baseball. But it is very popular on the youth level. Only basketball has more American players in leagues.

This does not take into account the hundreds and thousands of young people just kicking a ball around or kicking around a ball made of socks. That's how a young boy in Brazil named Edson Arantes do Nascimento got started. By the time he was 14, he was known as Pele. Not much later, he was known as the greatest of all soccer players.

"Soccer is a way of life in Brazil," Pele says. "It is something you do almost as soon as you can walk. It has a great history. It will have a great future because it is a beautiful game."

Pele in action with the New York Cosmos against the Chicago Sting

JOINING A SOCCER TEAM

How do you find out about joining a team in a soccer league? Many leagues find players through announcements at schools and in stores. Some may mail forms to your home. Others advertise on the radio and local television and in the newspaper. One of the best ways to find out about soccer leagues is from other players.

Leagues

Many leagues supply uniforms, shorts, awards, and a jersey. These items are included in the registration fee (perhaps $50 per child per year). Some leagues will help with the fees.

Players then are placed on teams. There they are taught the game by coaches who are volunteers. Coaches often hold practice once or twice a week. The practices often begin many weeks before a season. Coaches try to spend time with each player.

Soccer Equipment

Soccer players wear a jersey, shorts, knee socks, shin guards, and soccer shoes. The shoes usually have cleats on the bottom or sometimes studs. The cleats and studs must be at least one-half of an inch wide.

The goalie, the only player who can use his hands

Many players also wear knee pads, elbow pads, and, for boys, a protective cup. In recent years, young players have begun using mouthpieces. In some leagues, helmets or face masks are used, although they usually are discouraged.

"They can create problems for other players, with the opportunity to create injuries when, for instance, two players go for a head ball," says Eric Brummon, National Development Coordinator for the American Youth Soccer Organization. "I don't think it is necessary at this level. If someone felt it was necessary medically and could prove it would not be any potential harm for other players, then it could be allowed."

Goalies can wear pants and gloves, even a hat. And the jersey must be a different color from the other players so that a referee can easily spot the player allowed to use his or her hands.

The gloves are a key piece of equipment for a goalie. Goalies handle the ball a lot. Gloves should fit snugly and be replaced when they become worn.

Some items of basic equipment

Soccer shoes with cleats could cost $40 or more. Shin guards are usually about $10 or more. Goalie gloves range from about $7 to perhaps $80 or $90. The cost of a good soccer ball is usually around $25. Again, it can vary.

Taking care of your personal equipment is very important. The shoes, for example, should be cleaned after every game and practice. Any caked-on dirt or mud should be removed. Shoes that become worn, ripped, or don't fit well should be replaced right away.

CHAPTER 3

CONDITIONING AND WARM-UPS

Proper warm-ups are as important as learning the skills and rules of soccer. Without warm-ups, the chance of injury is strong.

"The need for conditioning is obvious," says Tony Martelli, an assistant coach at the U.S. Military Academy. "It is better for you so you can outrun a guy and outlast him.

"The warm-up before you start any kind of activity is important. You need a warm-up to stretch properly and begin to sweat. You might want to do a slow warm-up before you do any drills, so you are set for practice. Run around a little and kick a little to warm up. Then do drills as a team."

Warm-ups might seem like a waste of time to many young players. They want to play. But warm-ups are needed. They can be fun, too.

Start with jogging, stretching, and jumping. Maybe do some moving sideways or some sprinting. You can jump over a ball that is not moving. Then jump over a rolling ball. You can jump and pretend to hit the ball with your head.

Try standing in the net. Jump up and touch the bar across the top of it. Do it a few times. Then place your right foot against the

◀ Superstar Gian Luca Vialli of Italy on his way to another goal

goalpost. Stretch as far as you can toward the middle of the net. Do it on the other side of the net.

Don't get bored from warming up too long. Don't get tired, either. But make sure you have warmed up enough to be ready to play.

"If I am not ready, I could pull muscles, so I know it is important to warm up," says Jamie W., a 14-year-old player from Rockland County, N.Y. "But sometimes, if a coach works you out too long, there is no energy left for the game."

Of course, any player who stays in good shape all year has an edge. Maybe you can play other sports. You could do the same warm-ups year-round. It never pays to be lazy.

Also important is a well-balanced diet. Eating pizza or hamburgers at times is fine. But a steady diet of junk food is not. "You must have a mixed diet," Martelli says.

Basic jumping and stretching exercises. Learning to jump over a ball sideways and backward is useful.

Drinking water is also important. "If you don't drink water or other fluids, you can get tired quicker," adds Jamie. "Sometimes, it's good to splash water on your face to get cooler on a hot day."

Soccer is a fast and furious game. It requires and uses up a great deal of energy. You should feel your best to play your best. Do not fail yourself by failing to exercise and warm up for your games. Pay attention to your diet.

Basic jumping and stretching exercises

Georgio Chinaglia, one of the great superstars of the North American Soccer League

THE ELEVEN POSITIONS

The jobs of each player might be different from team to team. Defenders might never join the attack in one system. In another, they might move up often to try to score. But all teams use the same terms for each of the 11 positions on a field. In general, those positions are goalkeeper, defenders, midfielders, and forwards.

Some teams use four defenders. They are called fullbacks on the right and left side, sweeper in the middle in front of the goalie, and stopper in front of the sweeper. There usually are three midfielders. They are also called halfbacks (center, right, and left). Ahead of them are three attackers (left wing, right wing, and center forward). This system is called a 4-3-3.

Another setup, looking from your team's net upfield, is 3-4-3. In this system, the stopper does more offensively. Then there is one setup known as the 4-4-2, with one forward up front in the middle and the other roaming from side to side. There is even a 2-3-5. That was the classic formation used in most of the first half of this century.

Goalkeeper is the most important position. It is also the hardest to fill.

The most popular position is forward. Everyone likes to play forward because you score the most goals there.

FORMATIONS

The names of the positions vary according to the system or formation a team uses.

4-2-4 FORMATION
- **4** Defenders
- **2** Midfielders
- **4** Forwards

LW: Left Wing
CF: Center Forward
RW: Right Wing
IHB: Inside Halfback
LHB: Left Halfback
CHB: Center Halfback
RFB: Right Fullback
G: Goalie

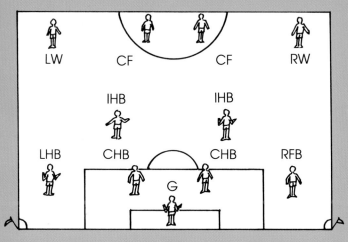

4-3-3 FORMATION
- **4** Defenders
- **3** Midfielders
- **3** Forwards

LW: Left Wing
CF: Center Forward
RW: Right Wing
LHB: Left Halfback
CHB: Center Halfback
RHB: Right Halfback
LFB: Left Fullback
CFB: Center Fullback
RFB: Right Fullback
G: Goalie

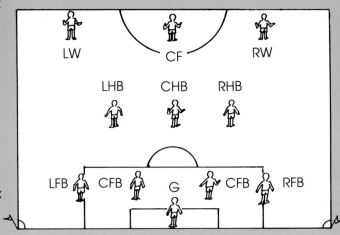

4-4-2 FORMATION
- **4** Defenders
- **4** Midfielders
- **2** Forwards

CF: Center Forward
LHB: Left Halfback
CHB: Center Halfback
RHB: Right Halfback
LFB: Left Fullback
CFB: Center Fullback
RFB: Right Fullback
G: Goalie

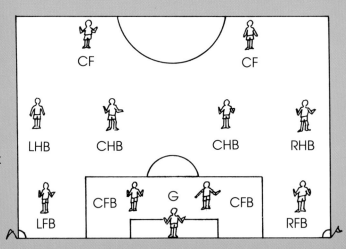

18

So, in quick review, there are goalies (also called keepers). There are forwards, sometimes called strikers. There are defenders (usually called fullbacks, sweepers, and stoppers). And there are midfielders (often called halfbacks). Let's look at each position. We will concentrate on the jobs of each position and the skills needed to play there.

The Goalkeeper

Goalkeepers really have just one job: to keep the ball out of their net. Goalies use anything and everything to stop opponents from scoring. They are, of course, the only players allowed to use their hands. But they can use their hands only inside the penalty area. That area is 44 yards wide and 18 yards long on a regulation-sized

Goalies must be quick with their feet.

field. For younger players, playing on a smaller field, the penalty area is smaller. The penalty area sometimes is called "the box."

"A goalie has to be aware of what's going on all over the field," says Tony Meola, the star keeper for the U.S. World Cup team in 1990. "He has to be able to think ahead of everyone and know when a team might break through."

Any goalie will tell you that making the diving stop or sliding kick-save looks great. But less flashy things are just as important. Teammates must know they can count on the goalkeeper. Like Meola, a goalie must be a leader. He must take charge at the defensive end of the field.

Many players fear playing goalie. After all, the ball is being kicked at them, not away. Overcoming that fear can be hard, especially for younger players.

SAFETY

It is especially important that goalies think about safety. In addition to wearing gloves for a better grip on the ball, they often wear padded pants, making it easier and more comfortable to slide safely. Safety also means learning to stop the ball with your hands or body and where to position yourself.

For a goalie to get comfortable, it helps to have somebody take shots at you. Start with soft, easy shots. That gives you confidence. Then work your way up to blocking harder shots. Then try high shots, curving kicks, and bouncers.

Most goalies stand just in front of the goal line. When an attacker is coming in from the side, a keeper "comes off the line." That means the goalie has to go out of the goal to challenge the shooter. You can "cut the angle," giving the shooter less of the net to aim for.

"The hardest thing for a goalkeeper to learn is when to come off the line and at what angle," says Meola. "That takes a lot of experience before it become natural."

As a keeper, always keep your body behind the ball. If the shot slips through your hands, you still might block it with your body. If the ball is rolling, field it the way an infielder takes a ground ball in baseball. Bend over with your feet together, or kneel to scoop it.

A goalie does not always need to catch the ball. Sometimes it is not smart to try to catch it. A goalie might need to punch it away, mainly on high shots. A goalie can also kick it on the run, especially when coming out of the net, or dive to stop a shot, and only deflect the ball away. It doesn't matter how you keep the ball out of the goal. It is just important that you do.

When you have made a save and are holding the ball, what is next? What are the choices? First, make sure you are set. Maybe you have made a hard save. Perhaps you are out of breath or your team is off-balance. Hold the ball for a few seconds and get ready.

Unlike hockey, for example, the goalkeeper in soccer does not have to get rid of the ball right away. With the ball in your hands,

Different ways a goalie
moves the ball

Two defenders fending off an attacker

you must direct traffic. You must send your teammates into areas where they can get your pass out or your punt more freely.

Often, if the fullbacks are free at the side, the goalie will roll the ball to them. The fullbacks will work it upfield. Sometimes, if a halfback or a defender is open farther upfield, a throw-out is wise. If you just want to clear the area, you might punt it way upfield. Do this especially when you spot an attacking edge somewhere.

Goalies should make a throw-out on a straight line so the ball is not in the air too long. The ball should be thrown with a motion like a hook shot in basketball. Make a throw-out while stepping toward the target.

On a punt, the goalie should drop the ball from the waist area and kick it from about knee height. A punt always should be high. Low punts are easy to intercept or block.

The Defenders

Just as with the goalie, a defender's first job is to stop an opponent from filling the net. But defenders (fullbacks on the outside and a sweeper and stopper in the middle) often join the attack, too.

Defenders generally are the biggest and strongest players. This is usually the case for the stopper and sweeper, the middle positions. The sweeper sweeps clear the defensive end of the field. The stopper tries to stop an attack before it gets too far and becomes too dangerous.

A defender can use many tactics. To be a defender, you must get between the goal and the opposing player. You should force an opponent toward the outside of the field. The sideline can help the defender, causing the attacker to try not to lose the ball out-of-bounds. This would give the ball to the defender's team. You need to stay close to an attacker. Do not give time or room to create a scoring chance. And do not block the view of your goalkeeper on shots. Defenders also are expected to block shots when they can. If a goalie is caught out of position, clear the ball away from the net. Don't use your hands or arms, of course.

It is important that defenders talk to each other. If the stopper (usually a defensive midfielder) or sweeper is forcing an attacker toward one side, then the fullback on that side must cover the middle. And he must let his teammate know he is doing so.

If a fullback is beaten to the outside and the attacker then cuts toward the net, the sweeper might come over to stop that attacker. The sweeper might yell to the fullback. The fullback would head toward the net to defend the area the sweeper has left.

A word often used on defense is "marking." This means covering a certain player. Each defender and halfback marks an opponent. A defender always must know which player is his to cover. If that opponent gets free, the defender must know whether a teammate can pick up the free player. If the teammate helps out, the beaten defender then must know immediately whom he must switch over to cover.

The Midfielders

If you are in great shape, can run all day and night, have a strong kick and plenty of speed, and want to help on offense and defense, then you have what it takes to be a midfielder. Midfielders are commonly called halfbacks.

Stamina is more important for a halfback than for anyone else in soccer. There simply is little chance to rest on the field. You are involved in all areas of the game. It has been said that in one game on a full-sized field, a halfback runs 8,000 yards. That means he has covered the length of the field 80 times!

Halfbacks serve as a link from the defensive players to the forward unit. In some systems, the halfbacks might stick to defense and almost never attack. Or they might be a constant part of the offense.

Outside halfbacks tend to stay on their sides of the field more than other players. They are asked to make all kinds of passes—short, long, high, on the ground. Outside halfbacks should have strong shots from long range.

Halfbacks have to adjust quickly. If two of them attack, the other halfback (or two halfbacks, depending on the number of them in the lineup) must stay back. Suppose an attack fails. The opponent gets the ball. The halfbacks must retreat quickly to the centerline. They must be ready to help the defense.

Halfbacks often handle throw-ins. Corner kicks and many planned plays center on the halfbacks.

The Forwards

Generally, a team's best scorer is placed in the center forward position. The fastest offensive players are on the wings. Most teams use three forwards. Rarely, if ever, are forwards asked to do anything but score.

Forwards are not expected to help on defense, except near the end of a game if their team is winning. They aren't even looked at to

Forward charging down the field to the goal ▶

create scoring chances as much as to take advantage of them.

Halfbacks and defenders might be the creators. They get the ball to the forwards in good position to attack. Most of a forward's time is spent in the opponent's penalty area. They often are surrounded by opponents. Forwards must be able to strike quickly and without much room.

It is important that a forward, especially a striker, be able to shoot strongly and accurately with both feet. "There are very few times

when you can think about what you want to do," the great Pele once said. "You must react right away, and you must be able to do it with your left or your right."

Very often, as the center forward, you will have your back to the net. You should be watching teammates and the flow of play. The center forward might cut toward the net for a pass. Then, you might need to volley (kick directly out of the air) or head the ball for a shot. So being skilled at shooting the ball out of the air in one motion is vital. So is sending it home with the head.

The wings aren't always such good scorers. They are needed to cross the ball (pass it high into the middle from the side). They must use their speed to get enough room, meaning they must be excellent dribblers.

Of all the positions, forward allows for the most initiative. Too many players waste scoring opportunities because they don't shoot enough. As a forward, when you get into decent shooting position, take the shot. That, too, is part of team play. When a forward is shooting the ball, he or she is taking care of the main job.

THE COACH'S JOB

A coach must be the boss of the team, in charge of all jobs:

- Putting the team together
- Arranging and running practices
- Setting up a playing schedule
- Taking care of transportation, practices and games
- Registering his players
- Deciding on strategy
- Coaching in a game

The Coach

Coaches must stress good sportsmanship and spirit. Often, they must also arrange for referees and linesmen. They check that the proper equipment is available and in good shape. They make sure the right first aid kits are on hand. They should know how to teach and how to play the game.

"A good coach has to encourage his players as well as teach them," says Nicole W., a 16-year-old high school player from Garner-ville, N.Y. "He has to command a lot of respect and, on higher level teams, he should appreciate the commitment players make."

The coach rallies his team.

Most coaches are volunteers. In high school and college, coaches generally are gym teachers. The main payback they get is the satisfaction of a job well done.

The Referee and Linesmen

Just as in other team sports, the person in charge on the field is carrying the whistle. He or she is the referee. The referee must make sure the nets are in shape. The referee checks to see the field is properly lined and playable. All players report to the referee, who makes sure they are registered and have proper uniforms. The referee then holds the coin toss before the kickoff.

During a game, the referee calls all fouls and penalties. He or she keeps the time and oversees all substitutions. Most beginner leagues have no limit for substitutions. Usually, they are made when play is stopped after a goal, for a foul, or when the ball has gone out-of-bounds.

Suppose a player makes a dangerous foul. Maybe the player shows poor sportsmanship. The referee can give the player a yellow card as a warning to behave. A second yellow card gets a player thrown out of a game. The referee can also hand out a red card, which means the player must leave the game right away.

The referee roams the whole field. The linesmen stay along the sidelines, one on each side, and carry flags. The linesmen call balls out-of-bounds. They signal offside calls. They also can signal illegal throw-ins and help the referee in calling fouls.

Heading the ball, a necessary skill

PLAYING SKILLS AND TECHNIQUES

As with any sport, the place to start in soccer is with the basics. Learning to shoot comes later. So does learning to head, dribble, and trap the ball. First, you must become comfortable handling the ball without using your hands.

"When I began to play, I used rolled up socks and rags," recalls Pele, the greatest player of all time, speaking of his first ball. "When I got to play with a ball, it was a very special thing for me."

Today, a ball almost always is available. What are the first drills that teach the young player how to use the ball?

Start with getting a feel for the ball by "juggling." That means controlling the ball in place first by simply kicking it back and forth from one foot to the other.

Once you have that feel, try juggling it in the air. Place the front of your foot on top of the ball. Pull it back toward you. As the ball rolls back, place the same foot under it. Lift the ball into the air. To keep it in the air, keep kicking it with the top of your foot. The ball should go only about head high or lower.

This is a fine exercise for becoming familiar with the ball. It helps your balance. It helps your eyes and feet work together. As you improve at this drill, add heading the ball, or include using your chest to keep the ball in the air and in your control. After you feel at ease with the ball, move on to other basic skills.

Kicking

Kicking is the most important part of soccer. Your chances of enjoying the sport are slim if you cannot kick the ball the right way.

In soccer, you don't just go out and swing your leg and kick the ball. There are right ways to kick. There are wrong ways, too.

Many new players use their toes for all kinds of kicks. But it is too hard to control the ball that way. Using the toes is fine, though, if you must clear the ball quickly.

The best way to kick the ball is with the instep. That is on the front side of your foot. You can control direction, distance, and height best that way.

Kicking accurately on the run is an important skill.

Say you are kicking with the right foot. Go to the ball so you can plant your left foot to the side of the ball. Then swing the right leg through the ball. Do not stop the foot once it hits the ball. Follow through. The foot should hit the ball with the instep very close to the ground.

The approach is important, too. Run naturally to the ball. Keep your eyes on it. You do not want to miskick or completely miss the ball. Whether the ball is rolling or is stopped, the basic skills of kicking are the same. Only the way you plant your non-kicking foot changes. With a moving ball, you must judge where to plant your foot when you and the ball reach each other.

Learn this skill, then you can do more things. You can get the ball up in the air by planting the non-kicking foot a bit behind the ball. Then bend the knee of your kicking leg more. Go ahead, try it.

Remember to keep your head steady when you are kicking. You can judge the kick all wrong if your head is moving and is out of position.

And remember that you have two legs. It is hard to use the left if you are right-handed. It is hard to use the right if you are a lefty. Try to learn to use either leg with equal ease.

One drill that often helps is to work only with your "off" leg. If you are right-handed, don't even place a shoe on your right foot during your workouts. That will make you think about using the shoed foot. Advanced players might do everything with their "off" leg during a practice. A right-footed player should practice or play on the left wing. That forces him or her to use the left leg more.

Dribbling

In basketball, you bring the ball up court by bouncing it. That is dribbling. In soccer, you do the same thing without using your hands. You dribble with your feet, mostly with the instep.

Again, it is important to use either foot. Dribbling with one foot all the time makes it harder to change direction. It is harder to control the ball. It will be easier for the other team to steal the ball.

The right way to dribble is to keep the ball close to you. Touch it every two or three steps. You can begin dribbling slowly. Speed up once you feel comfortable. Start by dribbling straight ahead. When you feel stronger at it, dribble to the side. Then dribble in a zigzag pattern.

Learning to dribble can be easier than learning to kick. You can work on it alone. You don't even need a lot of room. Drop the ball. Move ahead while dribbling as far as you can. Then turn around and do it again and again.

When ready, you can try dribbling "tricks." Maybe you could dribble between the legs of a defender, getting the ball on the other side of him. You could dribble backward a couple of steps. That might force a defender off-balance before you go past him.

Unlike kicking, your head doesn't need to be still when dribbling. Sometimes defenders look at your head. You can fake one way with it and dribble the other to get free. You also should look ahead rather than down at the ball. You can figure out where you want to go while you are dribbling.

Dribbling the ball

Trapping

Unless you are a goalkeeper, you can trap the ball with anything except your hands or arms. The chest trap often is used for high kicks you want to stop. Relax the chest just as you make contact with the ball. That deadens it. The ball should drop right down in front of you. Now kick it away.

The foot trap is made in several ways. One way is by lifting the front of the foot. Keep the heel down. That way, you can stop a rolling ball coming at you.

Suppose it is a low-bouncing ball. Lift the foot about six inches off the ground. Relax it when it touches the ball. The ball will stop near you, and you can control it.

Other traps are done with the shin, the thigh, and the head. To trap with the shin, hold your legs together, closed below the knee, as you crouch.

Passing

Pele is considered the greatest soccer player of all time. Why? Not only because of all the goals he scored. He was one of the game's greatest passers.

"I would get as much of a thrill from a pass I made to set up a goal as I did from scoring," he says. "If you are a good passer, it makes your teammates happier, because they are getting the chance to shoot from you."

Everyone loves to score goals. But the passes that set up goals are just as important. All passes are key parts of the game. Passing is the best way to move the ball along.

You can pass with the head, with your knee, or even with your chest if you are an advanced player. It is still wise for younger players to use the feet for passing.

A good pass should wind up at the feet of the receiver. That is not too hard when both players are not moving. But players always should be moving in a game. So figuring where to send the ball and how hard to pass it is difficult. It takes lots of practice with team-mates to master.

As in kicking, the best passes are made with the instep. You also can pass with the toes. You can pass with the outside of the foot or even with the heel if the passes are short ones. Think about using either foot, just as in kicking and dribbling.

Passing the ball

Heading

Heading is a very useful skill. Only the most advanced players even think about kicking balls when they are still in the air.

Some players are afraid of heading the ball at first. They think they will get hit in the face and get hurt. If a header is done the right way, though, it is quite safe.

Here is a drill to teach you the right way to do a header:

a) Hold the ball up to your head. Move your head to the ball. While holding onto the ball, hit it lightly with the center of your head.

b) Repeat this drill, hitting the ball a little harder each time.

c) Then, toss the ball slightly into the air. Watch it a few times. Try to figure out where your forehead must meet the ball as the ball comes down.

d) Now it is time to head it. Throw it up slightly. Put the middle of your forehead into it as the ball is dropping.

e) When you master this, try jumping into the ball. Make contact with your head. Your upper body should be moving forward into the ball. The neck muscles should move your head into the ball.

Heading the ball

f) Keep your mouth closed when jumping into the ball. It is dangerous to head the ball with your mouth open. You might bite your tongue.

g) Kick your legs behind you when you jump into the ball. This will give you more power.

Once you are better at heading, you will learn how to direct the ball with your head. You will even be able to hit it with the back of your head.

PLAYING THE GAME

Soccer can offer unlimited hours of fun. It also can provide some strong lessons for life. Through soccer, you learn how to work within a team for a common goal. You learn the importance of hard work. You are taught discipline. Players are taught to respect officials and other players. They also realize the value of being in good physical shape.

The idea of the game, of course, is to score more than the opponent. You move the ball down the field using your legs and your head. You try to get through the goalposts at the other end of the field, again using your legs and your head. Only one player, the goalkeeper, can use his hands.

The Setup

There are 11 players on each team for outdoor games. Some younger groups, especially beginners, might play with fewer than 11 on each team. (The number of players per team in indoor soccer changes with the size of the field.)

A full-size soccer field can be 100 yards long. It can be from 50 to 100 yards wide. The older you get, the bigger the field. For players in the 9 to 12 age group, fields are 100 yards long, 50 to 60 yards wide. Younger players use even smaller fields. The ball also is smaller for younger age groups.

Many leagues have beginners' programs for ages 5 or 6. Some will use fewer players (often six, seven, or eight on a side). The games

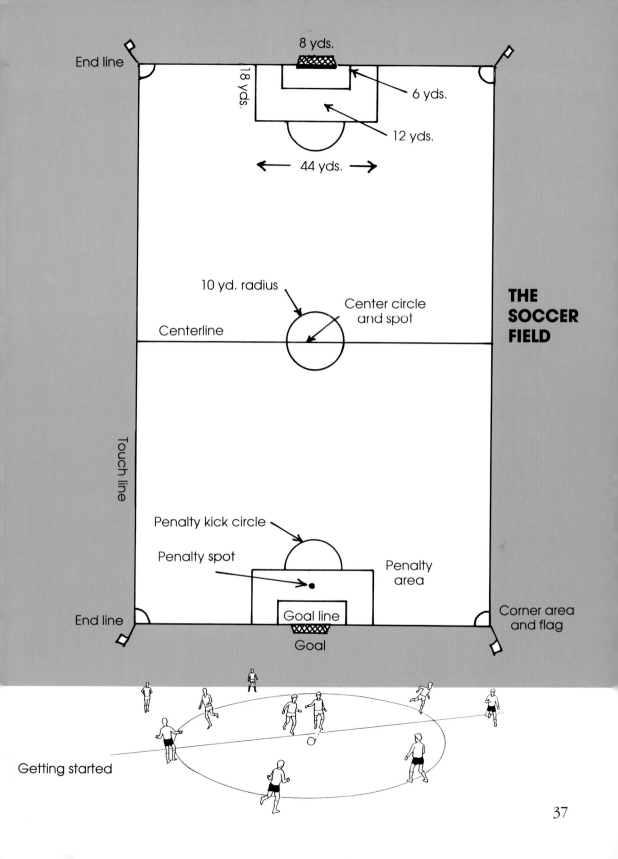

THE
SOCCER
FIELD

End line

8 yds.

18 yds.

6 yds.

12 yds.

44 yds.

10 yd. radius

Center circle and spot

Centerline

Touch line

Penalty kick circle

Penalty spot

Penalty area

Goal line

End line

Corner area and flag

Goal

Getting started

are shorter, perhaps only 40 or 45 minutes. Normal lengths for games can be from 50 minutes up to 90 minutes. The 90-minute game is for older players, high schools, colleges, and professionals.

The playing field has many lines on it. The centerline is where the kickoff is held at the start of each half, in overtime periods, and after a goal is scored. The centerline runs across the width of the field. It also is used to decide offsides, which will be explained in the stoppages section.

The penalty area is marked off by four lines. That includes the end line. The lines form a huge box. The box is 44 yards wide and 18 yards long on a full-size field.

Within the penalty area is a smaller box. This is called the goal area. It is 20 yards by 6 yards on a full field. Mainly it is a protected area for the goalkeeper.

The goal itself must be 24 feet long and 8 feet high for a full field. Again, it can be smaller for younger players using smaller fields.

Other markings include:

a) The center circle, where defending players cannot go during a kickoff.

b) The penalty arc at the top of the penalty area. This is used during penalty kicks. All players except the one taking the penalty kick and the goalie must be outside the arc (a half-circle).

c) The penalty spot, 12 yards from the goal. This is where the ball is placed for penalty kicks.

d) Smaller circles of about 1 yard at each corner of the field. The ball is placed in these smaller circles for corner kicks.

Flags are put at the corners of the field. These flags are supposed to be 5 feet high.

Getting Started

A coin toss usually decides which team kicks off and which end of the field each team defends. The teams switch ends for the second half. Some games, mainly in schools, are broken into four quarters.

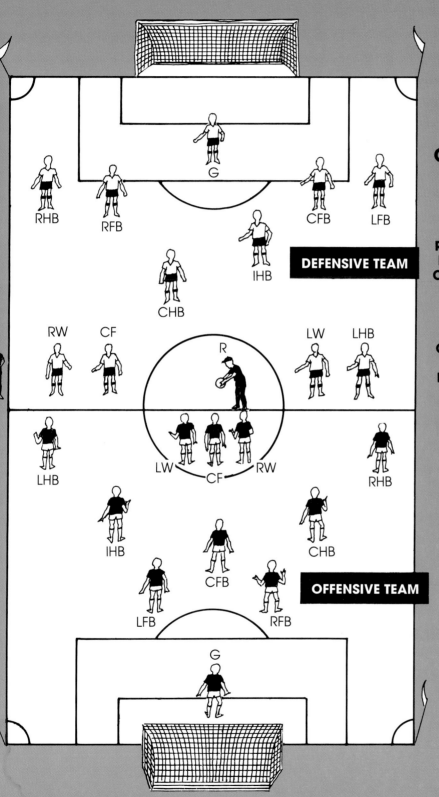

Getting Ready for the Game to Begin

G: Goalkeeper
RHB: Right Halfback
RFB: Right Fullback
CHB: Center Halfback (Stopper)
CF: Center Forward (Striker)
LFB: Left Fullback
CFB: Center Fullback (Sweeper)
LHB: Left Halfback
RW: Right Wing
IHB: Inside Halfback
LW: Left Wing

R: Referee
L: Linesman

DEFENSIVE TEAM

OFFENSIVE TEAM

Both teams line up on their side of the centerline for the kickoff. Usually, the team starting with the ball has a player kick it forward to a teammate. The teammate then passes it to another teammate. They try to get the ball upfield toward the opponent's goal. At the kickoff, the ball must move a distance at least its own size before another player can touch it.

Attacking

To win, of course, one team must score more than the other. The idea is to kick or head the ball into the opponent's net. Each score counts for one goal. A goal is scored when the ball is kicked or headed all the way across the goal line between the goalposts and under the crossbar.

You advance the ball toward the other team's net by dribbling, passing, or simply kicking the ball down the field. When you are close enough, you shoot, as outlined in Chapter 5. The better you get, the farther away from the net you might choose to shoot.

The team that does not have the ball tries to steal it. Then that team can start its own attack. Or the defending team just tries to clear the ball to the other end of the field.

Free Kicks and Penalty Kicks

The referee awards free kicks. They happen when a team is fouled or when an opponent breaks the rules in some other way, (such as hand ball — playing the ball with your hand — or using your body to stop an opponent from getting the ball). There are two types of free kicks: direct and indirect.

A direct free kick is given if one of nine moves that break the rules is made. Those nine are: kicking an opponent; jumping into an opponent; charging an opponent in a violent way; charging from behind, if it is violent or not; tripping; hitting or even trying to hit an opponent; pushing; holding; touching the ball with your hand. Directs are the most dangerous free kicks because they can be sent straight into the net.

Free kicks are awarded by the referee when a team is fouled.

Unless the direct kick is being taken very far from the net, the defenders form a wall. They stand right next to each other, so the shooter does not have an open shot at the goalie. The ball is in play once it is kicked. It can be cleared by the defense. Or it can be kicked again or passed by the offense.

When any of the nine fouls happens inside the penalty area, the referees award a penalty kick. Everyone except the shooter and goalie lines up outside the penalty arc. The ball is placed at the penalty spot 12 yards from the goal. The goalie cannot move until the kick is taken. If the penalty kick does not result in a goal, the ball is in play.

Indirect free kicks are given for unintentional fouls. They also are given for fouls not as dangerous as the nine just listed above. When an indirect is kicked, another player must touch the ball before it can go into the net. The defense again sets up a wall if the indirect is taken from close in. The offensive players can't go behind the wall. That would be offsides. The attackers often stand at the side of the wall or to the side of the shooter. The first attacker might tap the ball to a teammate. He might shoot it, a move many teams favor. Also, if the kick hits the goalie and drops in the net, it is a goal. Why? Because another player, the goalie, did touch the ball.

Stoppages

Play stops in many ways in soccer. But the clock stops *only* for injury or if the referee decides to hand out penalties.

If the whole ball goes over a sideline, the team that last touched it loses possession. The other team gets a throw-in. This is the only time that players other than goalkeepers use their hands.

When throwing the ball, the player must use both hands. The throw-in must come from behind and above the head. The player must keep both feet on the ground outside the sideline. If any of these rules are broken, the opposing team gets a throw-in. A player cannot score a goal on a throw-in. The ball must touch another player before it goes into the net.

What if the ball is kicked over the line at the end of the field, but not into the goal, by the attacking team? The defending team gets a goal kick. The goalie does not have to take this kick. Usually, a defender will make the goal kick.

The goal kick is a free kick up the field for the defending team. It is made from inside the goal area (the smaller box). All players must be outside the penalty area (the larger box). The ball cannot be touched by anyone until it is out of the penalty area.

Suppose the ball is sent over the end line but not into the net by the defending team. A corner kick is awarded the attackers. The kick is made from the corner nearest where the ball went out-of-bounds. It can be sent straight into the net for a goal.

The offside rule forbids teams from leaving players in front of their opponent's net. You are offside if you are the attacker and are past the centerline and there are no opponents between you and the goalie when the ball is played ahead by your teammate. The offside rule is not used if you get the ball off a corner kick, a goal kick, or a throw-in. When an offside is called, the defending team gets a free kick.

Corner kick

THINKING SOCCER

The hardest part of a sport isn't the physical part. In soccer, running and kicking sometimes are easier than the thinking. For younger players, there is less strategy. Players under 8 only have to know a few things. Defenders should know to stay back. Forwards have to attack. Midfielders are somewhere in the middle. Everyone should have fun.

When you get older, it becomes easier to understand tactics. It is important to learn why you do things. You have to be in certain places on the field.

Many strategies are mental and physical. When an attacker goes one-on-one with a defender, there are many moves to use. The attacker can use the body to shield the ball from the defender, dribble past the defender, pass the ball, or shoot.

But you must know when to dribble, when to pass, or when to shoot. These are mental skills. It takes time to develop them. After a while, they become automatic.

A defender must know when to go for the ball. When should you back off? When is it time to try a slide tackle? When do you stay on your feet? The defender learns to use the sideline or end line for help. He or she tries to force an attacker to the side of the field and

Knowing what to do at the right time is "thinking the game."

out-of-bounds. Maybe the attacker will lose the ball over the sideline or end line.

These tactics also can be used by all players working together. If a team has four halfbacks, the two inside halfbacks might attack. The outside halfbacks are used for defense, or vice versa.

Suppose you are one of three forwards. You might switch positions with another forward to confuse the defense. This can make an attacker free.

Team tactics are worked out by coaches. If the coach wants a defensive plan, a 4-4-2 setup is used. This means 4 defenders, 4 halfbacks, and 2 forwards, plus, of course, the goalkeeper. Teams using a 4-2-4 probably are looking for more offense.

If you totally understand your job on the field, you are thinking the game. First make sure you can do one position well. Then you can ask to try another. Do not try to learn too much too quickly. Pace yourself — mentally and physically.

FIND OUT MORE

Soccer programs are run by schools. They also are run by religious groups, YMCAs, and local clubs. Most have ties to the U.S. Soccer Foundation.

The USSF headquarters are in Chicago. There is a separate youth division. The USSF also has an amateur and professional division. For more information on the USSF's youth programs, you can write to:

The U.S. Soccer Federation
1811 South Prairie Avenue
Chicago, IL 60616

The U.S. Youth Soccer Association (USYSA) is the biggest group. Then comes the American Youth Soccer Organization (AYSO). Both have ties to the USSF.

The USYSA has 55 state associations. Some states have more than one. Nearly 1.5 million players are in USYSA. The USYSA can be contacted at:

The U.S. Youth Soccer Association
2050 North Plano Road
Suite 100
Richardson, TX 75082

The AYSO has local programs in 40 states. About 400,000 players ages 5 through 18 are involved. The AYSO is known for its rule that "everyone plays."

The AYSO helped make soccer popular. It started in the U.S. in 1984 in California. To contact the AYSO, write to:

American Youth Soccer Organization
5403 West 138th Street
Hawthorne, CA 90250

Some colleges run soccer in the summer. Players stay at the college for a few days and nights. They are taught the game. Some of these camps also teach other sports. They might have football, baseball, basketball, and swimming. But they usually have soccer, too.

Colleges advertise their summer sports programs for girls and boys in local newspapers and weekly shoppers' guides. You may also find information about soccer camps on your school bulletin board.

GLOSSARY

Center circle: A circle of 10 yards in radius at the middle of the field where kickoffs take place

Clearing: Kicking the ball away from the front of your team's net

Corner kick: The kick from the corner flag when the defending team has sent the ball over its end line. A goal can be scored on this kick.

Direct free kick: Awarded to a team when the opposing team has made one of nine serious fouls. A goal can be scored on this kick.

Dribbling: Advancing the ball with a series of short, soft, controlled kicks

Football: The international name for soccer. It is used in all countries, except the United States, Canada, and Australia, which have different kinds of football.

Forward: An attacking player

Foul: An illegal act that gives the offended team a free kick

Fullback: A defending player

Goal: The net into which players try to score

Goal area: The 6-yard by 20-yard part of the field in front of the net where goal kicks are taken

Goal kick: The kick given to the defending team after the attacking team sends the ball over the goal line but not into the net

Goal line: The line at both ends of the field between the goalposts

Goalkeeper: The only player allowed to use his or her hands. The goalkeeper (or goalie or keeper) defends the goal and can use his hands anywhere in the penalty area. The goalie can take four steps before he or she must get rid of the ball.

Hand ball: When players other than the goalie touch the ball with their arm or hand

Heading: Hitting the ball with your head as a shot or a pass, or to clear it

Indirect free kick: Awarded to a team when the opposing team has made a less serious foul. A goal cannot be scored on this kick; it must first be played by another player (including the goalkeeper).

Juggling: Hitting the ball by using different parts of the body to control it, a good training exercise

Kickoff: The start of the game, with the ball at the center spot. The ball must be kicked forward and must move a distance at least its own size. Kickoffs also are used after goals are scored.

Linesman: The official who carries a flag, stands on the sideline, and signals offsides and out-of-bounds plays

Midfielder (or halfback): A player positioned between the forwards and defenders, who plays both offense and defense

Offside: The foul committed when an attacker is past the centerline and does not have two defenders (including the goalkeeper) between the attacker and the goal when the ball is played

Own goal: When a player puts the ball into the opposing team's net, giving the opponent a score

Penalty area: The 18-yard by 44-yard area in front of the net. Goalkeepers can use their hands in this area.

Penalty kick: A direct free kick awarded because a serious penalty was committed in the penalty area. The shooter lines up at the penalty spot, 12 yards from the net. Only the goalie is also in the area, standing on the goal line. The goalie cannot move until the ball is kicked.

Red card: Handed to a player by the referee; the player is then out of the game for unsportsmanlike behavior.

Referee: The person who controls the game, keeping time, allowing substitutions, and calling all fouls

Save: A stop by the goalkeeper

Stopper: A defender who usually takes the place of a center midfielder

Striker: An attacking player

Sweeper: A defender, usually in the middle of the field, who is the last player on defense other than the goalie

Throw-in: A throw from the sideline after the opponent has sent the ball over the sideline. The throw-in is made with both hands above the head and both feet on the ground. You cannot score directly with a throw-in.

Trapping: Stopping the ball with your feet, chest, thighs, or head, then controlling it

Volleying: Kicking the ball on the fly when it is still in the air

Winger: An outside forward

Yellow card: The referee issues a yellow card to a player for a first minor

violation. A player can get only one yellow card; another violation results in a red card and immediate dismissal.

MORE WORDS TO KNOW

Advantage rule: A referee will stop play when a team commits a foul and gains an advantage from the foul. But if the foul by one team gives the opposing team the advantage, the referee won't blow the whistle.

Charge: Legal shoulder-to-shoulder contact to force a player off the ball

Chip: A short, high pass to lift a ball over a defender to a teammate

Crossbar: The bar running across the top of the goal

Dead ball: When the referee has stopped play, and the ball is not moving. All free kicks are taken on dead balls.

Instep: The best part of the foot to use for kicking. It is located at the front side of the foot.

Mark: To cover an opponent

Obstruction: When a player does not play the ball and uses his body to stop an opponent from getting the ball

Pitch: Another word for field

Slide tackle: Stopping an opponent who has the ball by sliding with legs out

FURTHER READING

Brown, Michael. *Soccer Techniques in Pictures*. Putnam, 1991

Rosenthal, Gary. *Soccer: The Game and How to Play It*. Lion, 1978

Ventura, Anthony. *Soccer, Play Like a Pro*. Troll Associates, 1989

Woods, P. *Soccer Skills*. EDC, 1987

INDEX

American Youth Soccer
  Association, 11, 45
Association football, 7-8
Attacking, 40, 43
Awards, 9

Baseball, 8
Basketball, 8
Brazil, 8
Brumman, Eric, 11

Charlton, Bobby, 4, 5
China, 5, 7
Chinaglia, Georgio, 16
Coach, 9, 26-27
Conditioning, 13-15
Corner kick, 42

Defenders, 17, 23-24, 43
Diet, 14
Dribbling, 29, 31-32, 40

England, 4-5, 7
Equipment:
  ball, 11
  cleats, 9
  costs, 11
  elbow pads, 10
  face mask, 10
  gloves, 11
  hat, 11
  helmet, 10
  jersey, 9, 11
  knee pads, 10
  knee socks, 9
  mouthpiece, 10
  pants, 11
  protective cup, 10
  shin guards, 9, 11
  shoes, 9, 11
  shorts, 9

studs, 9
uniforms, 9
Exercises, 14, 29-30

Field, 36-38
Football, 7, 8
Formation variations, 17, 18, 44
Forwards, 17, 24-26, 44
Fouls, 27-28, 40, 41
Fullbacks, 17, 18, 23

Goal, the, 38
Goal kick, 42
Goalkeepers (goalies), 19-23
Greece, 7

Halfbacks, 17, 18, 24
Hands, 11, 33
Heading, 29, 30, 34-35

Japan, 5

Kicking, 30-31, 40-41
Kickoff, 38

Leagues, 8, 9
Left wing, 17
Linesmen, 27-28
London Football Association, 7

Martelli, Tony, 13, 14
Meola, Tony, 20
Midfielders, 17, 24

Offside rule, 42

Passing, 33-34, 40
Pele (Arantes do Nascimento,
  Edson), 8, 26, 29, 33
Penalty area, 19, 20, 38, 41
Penalty kick, 40-41

Positions, 17-28
Punt, 22

Red card, 28
Referee, 11, 26, 27-28, 40, 42
Right wing, 17, 18
Roman Empire, 7
Rugby, 7

Shooter, 41
Soccer:
  history of, 7-8
  joining a team, 9-11
  playing the game, 36-42
  scoring, 41
  setup, 17, 18, 44
  stoppages, 42
  strategy, 43-44

Tactics (See Soccer: strategy)
Throw-in, 28, 42
Trapping, 29, 33

U. S. Military Academy, 13
U. S. Soccer Federation, 45
U. S. World Cup team, 20
U. S. Youth Soccer
  Organization, 45

Van Basten, Mark, 6
Vialli, Gian Luca, 12

Warm-ups, 13-15
Wembley Stadium, 4
World Cup, 4, 5, 8

Yellow card, 28